THE GOBLIN SHARK

By Sara Green

BELLWETHER MEDIA • MINNEAPOLIS, MN

Jump into the cockpit and take flight with Pilot books. Your journey will take you on high-energy adventures as you learn about all that is wild, weird, fascinating, and fun!

This edition first published in 2013 by Bellwether Media, Inc.

No part of this publication may be reproduced in whole or in part without written permission of the publisher. For information regarding permission, write to Bellwether Media, Inc., Attention: Permissions Department, 5357 Penn Avenue South, Minneapolis, MN 55419.

Library of Congress Cataloging-in-Publication Data

Green, Sara, 1964-
The goblin shark / by Sara Green.
    pages cm. – (Pilot. Shark fact files)
Audience: 8-12.
    Summary: "Engaging images accompany information about the goblin shark. The combination of high-interest subject matter and narrative text is intended for students in grades 3 through 7"–Provided by publisher.
Includes bibliographical references and index.
ISBN 978-1-60014-870-5 (hardcover : alk. paper)
1. Goblin shark–Juvenile literature. I. Title.
QL638.95.M58G74 2013
597.3–dc23
                        2012031537

Printed in the United States of America, North Mankato, MN.

TABLE OF CONTENTS

Goblin Shark: Identified 4

Goblin Shark: Tracked 12

Goblin Shark: Current Status 18

Glossary 22

To Learn More 23

Index.. 24

GOBLIN SHARK
IDENTIFIED

In the deep ocean, a pale pink shark floats motionless in the water. Hungry, the shark waits for prey to swim close by. Its long blade-like snout gives away its identity. This is the goblin shark, one of the most mysterious sharks alive. Suddenly, a squid swims near. In an instant, the shark **protrudes** its jaws. It looks like an alien! The shark bites the squid with its sharp teeth and pulls the meal into its mouth. Then the strange jaws disappear underneath the shark's long snout. They will stay hidden until the next attack.

The goblin shark inhabits the deep waters of the Pacific, Atlantic, and Indian Oceans. It has only been found in a few patchy areas near coasts. This includes the waters off of Japan, Australia, New Zealand, Portugal, and South Africa. A small population has also been reported off the coast of California.

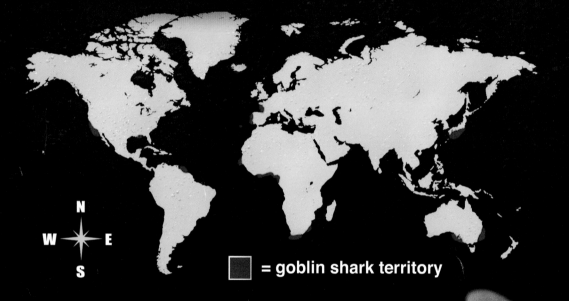

N
W E
S

☐ = goblin shark territory

Goblin sharks do not live in the open ocean. They live along **continental shelves** and near mountains that rise from the ocean floor. They swim to depths around 4,300 feet (1,300 meters) below the water's surface.

STRANGE CATCH

Japanese fishers caught the first known goblin shark in 1898. They named it *tenguzame*. In Japanese, this means "goblin shark."

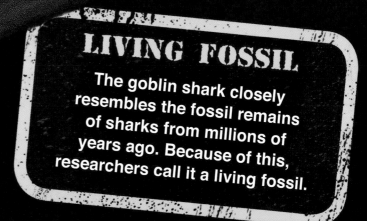

The goblin shark gets its name from its strange appearance. Its long, flat snout is its most recognizable characteristic. The jaws are more peculiar. They protrude when the shark hunts prey. The goblin shark has small eyes and a flabby body. Tiny blood vessels near the skin's surface give the shark its pale pink color. The body is covered with small, rough scales called **dermal denticles**. These protect sharks from injury and help them move smoothly through water.

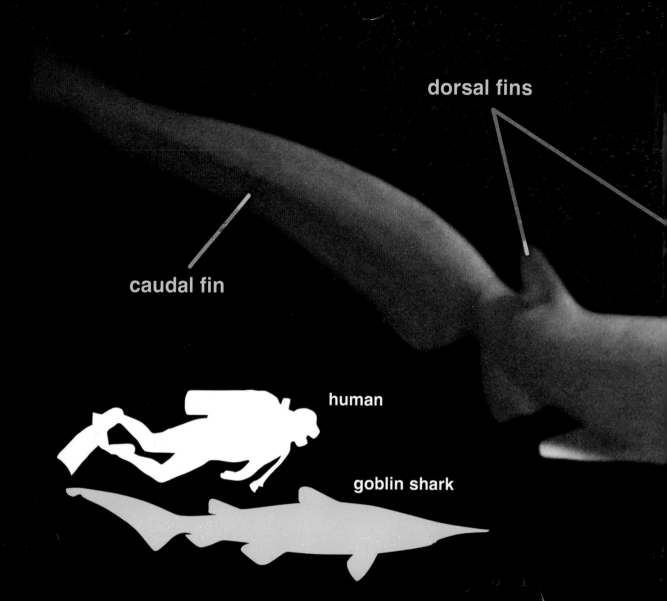

dorsal fins

caudal fin

human

goblin shark

Goblin sharks are usually between 10 and 12 feet (3 and 3.7 meters) long. The largest reported goblin shark was a female that measured 12.6 feet (3.8 meters) and weighed 463 pounds (210 kilograms). Up to a quarter of a goblin shark's body weight can come from its liver.

pectoral fin

Two **dorsal fins** keep the goblin shark balanced. The rounded **pectoral fins** help it steer. The goblin shark moves forward by swaying its long **caudal fin** from side to side. The shape of this fin suggests that the goblin shark is a sluggish swimmer.

GOBLIN SHARK
TRACKED

Nobody has ever seen a goblin shark give birth. They are probably **ovoviviparous** like other similar sharks. This means the mother lays eggs inside her body, and pups develop in the eggs. As they grow, they receive food from a **yolk sac** attached to their bodies. The eggs eventually hatch and the mother gives birth to live young.

Male goblin sharks are thought to **mature** when they are around 7.5 feet (2.3 meters) long. Scientists have not yet discovered when females begin to reproduce. They also have yet to learn how long goblin sharks live. With few opportunities to study the shark, it is difficult to find these answers.

Sunlight does not always reach the deep ocean where goblin sharks live. They must rely on keen senses to find prey in almost total darkness. Their long snouts are covered with jelly-filled holes called **ampullae of Lorenzini**. These allow sharks to sense the **electric fields** of nearby prey.

Lateral lines run the length of the goblin shark's body. They help the shark sense the movement of prey in the water. Many deep ocean creatures are **bioluminescent**. The goblin shark's small eyes may be able to detect their glowing bodies in the dark water.

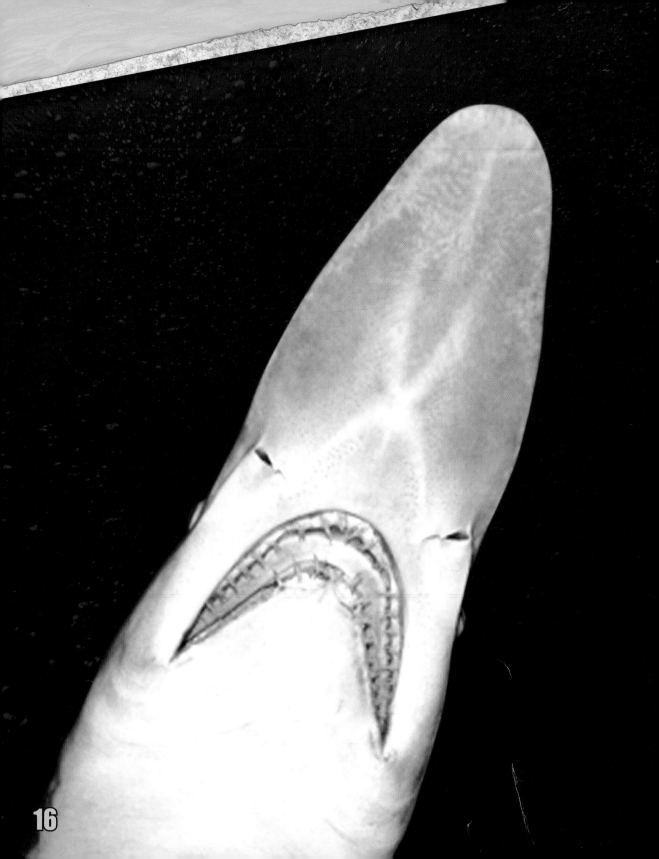

The goblin shark's mouth is full of sharp teeth arranged in rows. The front teeth are long and thin. They are well suited for catching slippery prey. The smaller back teeth are used to crush prey.

The goblin shark's large oil-filled liver keeps it **buoyant**. This allows it to float motionless in the water and wait for food. The shark's long, sensitive snout detects movement when prey swims near. Then its jaws protrude, and the shark sucks the prey into its mouth. Once the meal is caught, the goblin shark pulls its jaws back into its head. Squids, small fish, and crabs are thought to be the goblin shark's usual prey.

GOBLIN SHARK
CURRENT STATUS

Humans rarely dive to where goblin sharks live. This makes it difficult to estimate the number of goblin sharks in the world. Experts have reason to believe the population is not in danger. A few goblin sharks have been caught in **trawls** meant for other fish. Some of them ended up in research labs. Others were dried or smoked for food. Collectors like to purchase goblin shark jaws as trophies, but the species remains mostly unbothered by humans. For this reason, the International Union for Conservation of Nature (IUCN) has given the goblin shark a **least concern** rating.

CAUGHT OFF GUARD

After a 2003 earthquake in Taiwan, most nearshore fish had been wiped out. Fishers moved to deeper waters and met a catch they had never seen before. They pulled more than 100 goblin sharks up from the deep!

SHARK BRIEF

Common Name: **Goblin Shark**

Also Known As: **Elfin Shark**

Claim to Fame: **Long blade-like snout and jutting jaws**

Hot Spots: **Japan**

Australia

South Africa

California

Life Span: **Unknown**

Current Status: **Least Concern (IUCN)**

EXTINCT

EXTINCT IN THE WILD

CRITICALLY ENDANGERED

ENDANGERED

VULNERABLE

NEAR THREATENED

LEAST CONCERN

The goblin shark has kept many secrets. It cruises the deep ocean so far from human eyes that it may be able to keep them forever. Only a few people have ever seen this rare shark in its natural habitat.

As scientists study more of these fascinating sharks, their questions may slowly be answered. Until then, much of the goblin shark's life will remain as dark and mysterious as the waters around it.

GLOSSARY

ampullae of Lorenzini—a network of tiny jelly-filled sacs around a shark's snout; the jelly is sensitive to the electric fields of nearby prey.

bioluminescent—able to give off light

buoyant—able to float

caudal fin—the tail fin of a fish

continental shelves—flat underwater extensions of continents that drop to the ocean floor

dermal denticles—small tooth-like scales that cover some types of fish

dorsal fins—the fins on the back of a fish

electric fields—waves of electricity created by movement; every living being has an electric field.

lateral lines—a system of tubes beneath a shark's skin that helps it detect changes in water pressure

least concern—at a low risk of becoming endangered

mature—to become old enough to reproduce

ovoviviparous—producing young that develop in eggs inside the mother's body; ovoviviparous animals give birth to live young.

pectoral fins—a pair of fins that extend from each side of a fish's body

protrudes—juts forward

trawls—strong nets that are dragged along the ocean floor

yolk sac—a sac of nutrients that feeds some animals as they develop inside their mothers

TO LEARN MORE

At the Library

Bradley, Timothy J. *Paleo Sharks: Survival of the Strangest.* San Francisco, Calif.: Chronicle Books, 2007.

Lynette, Rachel. *Bluntnose Sixgill Sharks and Other Strange Sharks.* Chicago, Ill.: Raintree, 2012.

Wilsdon, Christina. *Sharks.* Pleasantville, N.Y.: Gareth Stevens Publishing, 2009.

On the Web

Learning more about goblin sharks is as easy as 1, 2, 3.

1. Go to www.factsurfer.com.

2. Enter "goblin sharks" into the search box.

3. Click the "Surf" button and you will see a list of related Web sites.

With factsurfer.com, finding more information is just a click away.

INDEX

ampullae of Lorenzini, 14
bioluminescence, 15
buoyancy, 17
coloring, 4, 9
continental shelves, 7
dermal denticles, 9
eggs, 12
electric fields, 14
females, 10, 11, 12, 13
fins, 10, 11
fishing, 7, 11, 18, 19
giving birth, 12
hot spots, 20
International Union for
Conservation of Nature
   (IUCN), 18, 20
jaws, 4, 9, 11, 17, 18, 20
lateral lines, 15
life span, 13, 20
living fossil, 9

males, 13
maturing, 13
population, 6, 18
prey, 4, 9, 14, 15, 17
pups, 12
reproduction, 12, 13
senses, 14, 15, 17
size, 10, 11, 13
status, 18, 20
teeth, 4, 17
territory, 6, 7, 20
threats, 18